Senses

Sniffing and Smelling

Author's Note

I have worked alongside young children for more than 40 years.
Over this period I have learned never to be surprised at their perceptive
comments about the physical world in which they live. Many of their
observations ("Have you seen the crinkles in the elephant's trunk?"
"How do seeds know which is their top and which is their bottom?")
indicate keen observation and an intuitive use of the senses of taste,
touch, sight, smell, and hearing.

The sense-dependent nature of the young child should come as no
surprise to parents and teachers. In the early years of life images
provided by the senses shape our interpretation of our surroundings
and lay the foundations upon which subsequent learning is built.
The ideas of hot and cold, far and near, quiet and loud, sweet and sour,
soft and hard are developed through the interaction of the child with his
or her immediate environment. This interaction encourages observation
and questioning which in turn leads to talk and the extension and
deepening of language.

This book (like its companions in the series) is a picture book which seeks
to encourage both looking and talking. The text may be read by child or
adult. Alternatively it may be ignored, the pictures alone being used to
trigger an exploration of the child's own insights.

Published by Raintree Steck-Vaughn Publishers, an
imprint of Steck-Vaughn Company, a subsidiary of
Harcourt Brace & Company

Editors: Helen Lanz, Shirley Shalit
Art Director: Robert Walster
Project Manager: Gino Coverty
Designer: Kirstie Billingham
Photo Researchers: Sarah Snashall

Library of Congress Cataloging-in-Publication Data
Pluckrose, Henry Arthur.
Sniffing and smelling / by Henry Pluckrose.
    p. cm. -- (Senses)
Summary: Introduces the basic concept of smell and
how it affects our lives.
ISBN: 0-8172-5228-2
1. Smell--Juvenile literature. [1. Smell. 2. Senses and
sensation.] I. Title. II. Series: Pluckrose, Henry Arthur.
Senses.
QP458.P553 1998
612.8'6--dc21   97-30962
                                                           CIP
                                                           AC
Printed in Malaysia and bound in the United States
1 2 3 4 5 6 7 8 9 0 LB 01 00 99 98 97

Picture credits
Commissioned photography by Park Street: cover; Steve Shott: 4, 5, 11, 21. Researched photography: Bruce
Coleman Ltd 14 (P. Clement), 18 (T. Buchholz), 27; Eye Ubiquitous 8-9 (D. Safhahevan); Images Colour Library
10; Rex Features 29 (Mourlhion); Robert Harding 23 (Schmied); PhotoEdit 31 (D. Young-Wolff); New England
Stock Photo 6 (J. Rothan/V. Jackson); Spectrum Colour Library 17 (M. Birch); Tony Stone 12 (T. Craddock), FPG
International 13 (B. Losh), 16 (P. Cade), 19 (R. Sutherland), 20 (A. Blake), 30 (S. Fellerman); Zefa 15, 24, 28.

Senses

Sniffing and Smelling

by Henry Pluckrose

RSVP

RAINTREE
STECK-VAUGHN
P U B L I S H E R S
The Steck-Vaughn Company

Austin, Texas

4

When you breathe,
your nose helps you tell
what smells and odors
are carried in the air.

Some smells are
easy to recognize,
like the heavy smell
of smoke and fire.

Some smells are so exciting
that we can almost taste them,

like the mouthwatering smell
of fresh bread.

Some smells are sweet.
Does a banana, an apple,
or an orange
taste like its smell?

There are many different smells
in a garden—
the clean smell of cut grass,
the tangy smell of mint,
the perfume of roses.

Odors in the woods
change with the seasons.
In the fall they are rich with
the moldy smell of damp earth
and fallen leaves.

Farms have many smells—
the warm smell of farm animals,
the rich smell of plowed earth,
the sweet smell
of harvested crops.

Along the coast the air
smells and tastes of salt.
Boats in the harbor
smell of gas and oil,
saltwater, and fish.

Not everybody
likes the same smells.
Do you like the smell
of cheese?
What about garlic?

Not all smells are pleasant.
Rush hour brings traffic to a halt.
The air is heavy with the
exhaust of cars, trucks, and buses.
Sometimes it gets hard to breathe.
The air smells bad.

Our sense of smell
tells us about the world
in which we live,
our environment.
A polluted river is dirty.
It has a sickly smell.
The smell reminds us that
we must take better care
of our environment.

Animals have a sense of smell.
A mother sheep recognizes
her lamb by its smell.
Her lamb has a different smell
from all the others in the flock.

Most dogs have
a very keen sense of smell.

Some dogs are used to help the police. They sniff and sniff and find things the police are looking for.

We have a sense of smell,
but we smell, too.
What things do people use
to make them smell sweeter?

Investigations

This book has been prepared to encourage the young user to think about the sense of smell and the way in which the nose interprets the multitude of "scents" that hang in the air we breathe.

Each picture spread creates an opportunity for talk. Sharing talk with a sympathetic adult plays an important part in the development of a child's understanding of the world. Through the subtlety of language, ideas are formed, questioned, and developed.

The theme of smell might be explored through questions like these:

⭐ The nature of smell. What do we mean by smell? Are there some smells which you immediately recognize? Which smell do you recognize most easily? What do you "see in your mind" when you sniff a familiar smell?

⭐ Smells pleasant, smells unpleasant (pp 6-9, 20-21). Which things do you like to smell—or like smelling least of all? Does everybody (in your family/class) find the same smells attractive?

⭐ Defining smell (pp 12-17). What words can we use to define a smell? What do we mean by a "heavy" smell, a "sweet" smell, a "sour" smell? Can a smell be described as hot, cold, damp, dry—or warm? Can a smell be frightening or comforting?

⭐ Messages from smells (pp 22-25). The way in which we live often pollutes our environment. The unpleasantness of some smells (like car exhaust) provides a warning of how careful we must be to maintain the quality of the air we breathe. What problems are caused when the air becomes too heavily polluted? How does air pollution affect health?

⭐ Unity of the senses (pp 8-9, 18-19). It is important to talk about the way our senses work in harmony. What things can we identify simply through the sense of smell?

⭐ The world of nature (pp 26-29). Like us, animals possess a sense of smell. Watch a dog or a cat. On what occasions can you *see* a domestic pet using the sense of smell?